Swan

Series "Fun Facts on Birds for Kids"

Written by Michelle Hawkins

Swan

Series "Fun Facts on Birds for Kids"

By: Michelle Hawkins

Version 1.1 ~January 2021

Published by Michelle Hawkins at KDP

Swans do not find their mate till they are around seven years of age.

A Swan nest is made up of leaves and twigs.

In the duck goose family, Swans are the largest bird.

The most famous ballet in the world is called "Swan Lake" by Tchaikovsky.

Swans wingspan can be up to ten feet.

Swans are the most faithful bird on the animal planet.

Swans are known for their long neck.

A fear of swans is called Cynophobia.

Swans live on average twenty to thirty years, depending on their breed.

Swans will lay three to eight eggs at one time.

Swans will mate for life.

A Black Swan will only use one leg to swim.

Baby Swans will stay with the mother till they are six months of age.

Predators of Swans are the Racoon, Wolf, and Humans.

Swan eggs are black and gray.

Swans are not known to live in tropical environments.

Some Swans migrate while others do not.

Swans are seen as freedom, kindness, and purity.

Swans have webbed feet to enable them to swim.

Swans can run on land up to twenty-two miles per hour.

Swans eat mostly plants, seeds, and fruit with an occasional fish.

To kiss, Swans will touch their beaks together, which will make the heart sign.

Swans are known as a graceful animal.

Six percent of Swans will divorce due to nesting issues.

A beak on a Swan looks like a saw.

With the Swans beak, they can eat food.

Swans in water can swim up to one and a half miles per hour.

Swans can fly up to sixty miles per hour.

Swans are very protective and will attack if provoked.

A Northern Hemisphere Swan is white with an orange beak.

There are no Swans in Africa or Antarctica.

A Swan high five is when they flap their wings.

Swans will nest from April to July.

Southern Hemisphere Swans are white and black, with their beak being either black, orange, or red.

Swans are very intelligent birds, more than even dolphins.

Swans can weigh up to thirty pounds.

Swans will fly in a V formation.

Swans are known for their trumpet sound.

Swans are one of the largest birds that fly in the world.

Two Swan necks entwined is a universal symbol of love.

The word Swan means to sing or sound.

A female Swan is called Pens.

A male Swan is called a Cob.

A baby Swan is called a Cygnet.

A group of wild Swans is called a Herd

A group of captive Swans is called a Fleet.

Swans live in freshwater.

Swans will remember how you treat them in the future.

Swans, on average, have 25,000 feathers on their body.

A Swan is considered an adult at the age of four.

When Swans sleep on lang, they will sleep standing up on one leg.

A significant threat to Swans is water pollution.

Swans can be up to five feet long.

Swans will lay on their nest for up to six weeks before the eggs hatch.

Swans are found mostly in Australia, New Zealand, and South America.

Swans are a part of the Anatidae family.

Black Swans are found only in Australia and New Zealand.

Swans can sleep on both water and land.

There are seven different types of Swans in the world.

Swans represent elegance.

You will mostly find Swans in lakes, ponds, and rivers.

Swans can fly up to sixty miles per hour.

Find me on Amazon at:

https://amzn.to/3oqoXoG

and on Facebooks at:

https://bit.ly/3ovFJ5V

Other Books by Michelle Hawkins

Series

Fun Facts on Birds for Kids.

Fun Fact on Fruits and Vegetables

Fun Facts on Small Animals